Happy Venture
Playbook Three

Now for some Stories

FRED J. SCHONELL
and PHYLLIS FLOWERDEW

Illustrated by Jack Keay
and William Semple

OLIVER AND BOYD: EDINBURGH

Note on the Revised Edition

HAPPY VENTURE was conceived and has been validated as a basic teaching method, and as such has proved outstandingly successful. Our language is a living one, however, and so certain expressions appearing in the original edition have now gone out of use.

Before his death in 1969, Professor Schonell was actively engaged in discussion with the publishers about the revision of the entire series. Unfortunately he was not able to undertake this before he died.

After consultations with practising teachers throughout the country and abroad, it became apparent to the publishers that the principles on which the series was based had not altered, but that minor changes to up-date the text could be made without affecting the well-tested structure of the series.

Accordingly, in this book, teachers will find:
new illustrations where main characters appear and of diesel engine; minor alterations to text, e.g. 'new pennies' substituted for 'shillings'; and consequent changes to Word List.

The publishers acknowledge the help and advice of Miss Angela Ridsdale of Toorak Teachers' College, Malvern, Victoria, Australia, in the preparation of the Australian edition of this series.

The publishers acknowledge the help and advice of Miss Angela Ridsdale of Toorak Teachers' College, Malvern, Victoria, Australia, in the revision of this series.

Contents

The Brave Little Duck

One morning in winter
  the wind went out to blow.

" Oo, oo, oo," he said.
" I will blow. I will blow.
I will make the ground cold.
I will put ice on the pond."

So he blew and he blew
  and he blew.

Soon he saw a little duck
  on the pond.

" Quack, quack," said the duck.
" I will swim.   I will swim.
I will swim to keep warm."

" Oo, oo, oo," said the wind.
" I will make the ground cold.
I will put ice on the pond.
I will not leave one hole
  where you can swim."

So he blew and he blew
  and he blew.
He made the ground cold.
He put ice on the pond.
And he did not leave one hole
  where the duck could swim.

" Quack, quack," said the duck.

" Now there is no water
in the pond. It is all ice
and I cannot swim."

So he walked to the grass
at the side of the pond,
and he was very cold.

" Oo, oo, oo," said the wind,
and he blew away.

In the morning the wind
    went out to blow again.
He blew over the cold ground.
He came to the pond
    where he had put the ice.

There he saw the little duck.

The little duck was cold,
    but he had made a little hole
    in the ice,
    and he was swimming, swimming

" Quack, quack," said the duck.
" I will swim. I will swim.
I will swim to keep warm."

" Oo, oo, oo," said the wind.
" I will make the ground colder.
I will put more ice on the pond.
I will not leave one hole
    where you can swim."

So he blew and he blew
   and he blew.

He made the ground colder.

He put more ice on the pond.

And he did not leave one hole
   where the duck could swim.

" Quack, quack," said the duck.
" Now there is no water
   in the pond.
My little hole is all ice again,
   and I cannot swim."

So he walked to the grass
   at the side of the pond,
   and he was very cold.

" Oo, oo, oo," said the wind,
   and he blew away.

In the morning the wind
  went out to blow again.
He blew over the cold ground.
He came to the pond
  where he had put the ice.
There he saw the little duck.
The little duck was cold,
  but he had made
  another little hole in the ice,
  and he was swimming, swimming

" Quack, quack," said the duck.
" I will swim. I will swim.
I will swim to keep warm."

" Oo, oo, oo," said the wind.
" I will make the ground colder,
    and colder, and colder still.
I will make the ice thicker,
    and thicker, and thicker still.
I will not leave one hole
    where you can swim."

So he blew and he blew
    and he blew.
He made the ground colder,
    and colder, and colder still.
He made the ice thicker,
    and thicker, and thicker still.
And he did not leave one hole
    where the little duck could swim.

" Quack, quack," said the duck.
" Now there is no water
in the pond. My little hole is
all ice again, and I cannot swim.
So he walked to the grass
at the side of the pond,
and he was very cold.

" Oo, oo, oo," said the wind,
and he blew away.

In the morning the wind
went out to blow again.
He blew over the cold ground.
He came to the pond
where he had put the ice.
There he saw the little duck.
The little duck was cold,
but he had made
another little hole in the ice,
and he was swimming, swimming

" Well ! " said the wind.
" What a brave little duck.
I cannot beat him.
I will leave him."

He left the brave little duck
    swimming, swimming,
    swimming to keep warm.

So the wind blew away
    and left the brave little duck
    swimming in the hole
    in the ice.

White Horse and
Brown Horse

One day little brown horse
   said to little white horse,
" It is a fine morning.
The sun is shining.
Tell me what you can see
   today."
Little white horse
   said to little brown horse,

" I am look, look, looking
and I can see
children going to school.
I can see boys and girls
running and dancing
on the way to school."

Then little white horse
said to little brown horse,
" It is a fine morning.
The sun is shining.
Tell me what you can see
today."

Little brown horse
said to little white horse,
" I am look, look, looking
and I can see
an engine and a coal truck
standing in the station,
standing still in the station."

11

Then little brown horse
  said to little white horse,
" It is a fine morning.
The sun is shining.
Tell me what you can see
  today."

Little white horse
  said to little brown horse,
" I am look, look, looking
  and I can see a fire engine
  coming up the hill,
  coming up the hill very fast."

White horse and brown horse
  looked at the children
  going to school.

They looked at the engine
  and the coal truck
  in the station.

They looked at the fire engine
    coming up the hill.
Then the children went into
    school and were gone.
The engine and the coal truck
    went out of the station
    and were gone.
The fire engine went
    over the hill and was gone.

Then little brown horse
    said to little white horse,
" What can you see now ? "

Little white horse
said to little brown horse,
" I can see a field,
a field of green grass.
I am going to run and trot
and jump in it."

So little white horse
went to run and jump and
trot round the green field.
And little brown horse
went after him to run
and jump and trot
round the green field too.

The Red Dancing Shoes

Sally liked dancing.
She danced
in the house.

She danced
in the garden.

She danced
on the way
to school.

And on Saturday
she went dancing
with other girls.

So Saturday was the day
she liked best of all.

Now when Sally was six,
   her father gave her
   some shoes.

They were little.
They were red.
They were dancing shoes.

" Oh ! " said Sally,
   " how nice they are ! "

She put them on
   and danced
   round the table.

She danced
   in the house.

She danced
   in the garden.

" I can dance very well
   in my little red dancing shoes,'
   she said.

But one Saturday
   after dancing
   Sally lost one of her shoes.

She went back at once
   to look for it.
She looked along the road.
But the red dancing shoe
   was not there.
She looked in the park.
But the red dancing shoe
   was not there.

For the little red dancing shoe
   was lost, lost, lost.

And Sally was very sad.
She was so sad
   that she did not dance at all.

She walked in the house.
She walked in the garden.
She walked on the way to school.

But where was
   the little red dancing shoe ?

Well, first a cat saw it
   on the road.

" One shoe is no good,"
   she thought.
So she picked it up
   and took it along with her.

Then she left it
   on the road again.

18

Soon a boy came by.
He saw the little
   red dancing shoe.

" One shoe is no good,"
   he said.

So he kicked it.
He kicked it
   a long way.

He kicked it
   up the road
   and down the road.

Then he left it
   by a shop.

19

Soon the old man from the shop
   saw the little red dancing shoe.

" Some little girl
   has lost a shoe," he thought.
" I will put it in my shop.
Then she may see it."

So he picked up
   the little red dancing shoe
   and put it in his shop.

He put it with the eggs
   and the sugar
   and the butter.

Then one day
   Sally went that way.

She stopped to look
   in the shop.

She saw eggs and sugar
   and butter.

And she saw a shoe !

It was little. It was red.
It was her dancing shoe.

" Oh ! " said Sally.
" There is my shoe ! "

She went into the shop
     and the old man
     gave her the shoe.

So Sally was happy again,
     and she danced
     and she danced
     and she danced.

21

The Silver Ball

Once upon a time
   there was a silver ball
   in a silver box
   in a big house by the sea.

One day the man of the house
   took the silver ball
   out of the silver box,
   and walked down to the sand.

There he saw some children.
He saw boys and girls
 running and jumping
 on the sand.

He called them to him
 and held up the silver ball.
" Look at this silver ball,"
 he said.
" See it shining
 in the sun.

Now, I am going to say,
 ' One, two, three,'
 and I am going
 to throw
 the silver ball.

I shall throw it
 up in the sky.

I shall give twenty new pennies
  to the boy or girl
  who gets the ball
  and brings it to me."

" Oh," said the children.
" That will be fun."

" Oh," said John,
" I should like
  to get
  the silver ball."

" Oh," said Jack,
" I should like
  to get
  the silver ball."

" Oh," said Sally,
" I should like
  to get
  the silver ball."

" So should we,"
   said the other children.
" We should all like
   to get the silver ball."

The man smiled
   and held up the silver ball.
" Here it is," he said.
" See it shining in the sun.
Now !   One, two, three ! "

When he said " three,"
   he threw
   the silver ball.

He threw it
   high up in the sky.

The children
   held up their hands.

They ran and jumped
   and jumped and laughed.

They all tried and tried
to catch the silver ball.
But no one could catch it.

The silver ball fell down,
down on the sand.

First John picked it up,
but he lost it again.

Then Sally put her hand
on it,
but she lost it again.

Jack kicked it,
but he lost it again.

All the children tried
to get the silver ball,
but it rolled away.

It rolled over the sand
and down to the sea.

" Stop it," cried the man,
   running after it.
But he could not stop it.

" Stop it," cried the children,
   running after it.
But they could not stop it.

The silver ball
   rolled down the sand
   and into the sea.

It sailed
  on the sea
  like a silver boat,
  and no one could get it.

" Oh ! " said the man.
" It has gone."

" Oh ! " said the children.
" It has gone."

So no one got the silver ball
  and no one had
  the twenty new pennies.

In the morning,
  just as the sun got up,
  a little boy called Peter
  went walking on the sand.
No one was about.

Peter looked at the sun
   dancing on the sea.
He looked at the sea
   running up on the sand.

Then he saw something.
He saw a silver ball.
It sailed on the sea
   like a silver boat.
It had been out all night
   and now it was coming back.

Peter sat down to wait.
" I will wait and wait
   for it," he said.

The sea ran up on the sand
and back again.
It ran up on the sand
and back again.
The silver ball
was coming nearer.
It was coming nearer
and nearer and nearer.

Peter took off his shoes
and ran into the water.
The silver ball came nearer
and nearer.

At last it came so near
that Peter could get it.
He put out his hand
and picked up the silver ball.

Then he put on his shoes,
and he ran up the sand
to the big house.

He gave the silver ball
   to the man of the house.

" Thank you," said the man.
" Thank you very much."

He gave Peter twenty new pennies,
   and he put the silver ball
   in the silver box
   in the big house by the sea.

The Magic Ring

Once upon a time
  there was a man
  who had a magic ring.

He put it in a little box,
  and put the box on the table.

He said to his wife,
" The ring can give us one wish,
  but only one.
What shall we wish for ? "

His wife thought and thought.
Then she said,
" It would be nice to have a cow,
  a fine, fat cow.
Let us wish for a cow."

The man thought and thought.
Then he said,
" Yes. It would be nice
  to have a cow, a fine, fat cow.
But if we work very hard
  all the time,
  we can buy a cow.
Then we will not
  have to wish
  for that."

So they left the magic ring
  in the little box.
They left the little box
  on the table,
  and they worked very hard
  all the time.
Then they bought a cow.

" Now," said the man to his wife,
  " let us have the wish.
The ring can give us one wish,
  but only one.
What shall we wish for ? "

His wife thought and thought.
Then she said,
" It would be nice to have
  a horse, a fine big horse.
Let us wish for a horse."

The man thought and thought.
Then he said, " Yes.
It would be nice to have
  a horse, a fine big horse.
But if we work very hard
  all the time,
  we can buy a horse.
Then we will not have
  to wish for that."

So they left the magic ring
  in the little box.
They left the little box
  on the table,
  and they worked very hard
  all the time.
Then they bought a horse.

" Now," said the man to his wife,
  " let us have the wish.
The ring can give us one wish,
  but only one.
What shall we wish for ? "

His wife thought and thought.
Then she said,
" It would be nice
  to have a cart
  for the horse to pull along.
Let us wish for a cart."

The man thought and thought.
Then he said,
" Yes. It would be nice
  to have a cart
  for the horse to pull along.
But if we work very hard
  all the time,
  we can buy a cart.

Then we will not have
  to wish for that."
So they left the magic ring
  in the little box.
They left the little box
  on the table,
  and they worked very hard
  all the time.
Then they bought a cart.

So the time went by,
and now and then
the man and his wife
looked at the magic ring.

Each time they said,
" Now let us have the wish,
for we want

a pig,

a sheep,

a rabbit,

a hen,

a duck,

a dog,

a kitten,

and lots of other things."

But each time they said,
" If we work very hard
  we can buy these things.
Then we will not have
  to wish for them."

So the man and his wife worked
  all the time.
They worked very, very hard.

And soon they had bought
  a cow, a horse, a cart, a pig,
  a sheep, a rabbit, a hen,
  a duck, a dog, a kitten,
  and lots of other things.

So they did not have
  the wish.
They never, never, never
  had the wish at all.

The magic ring
   was left in the little box
   on the table.
And the man and his wife
   were as happy as could be.

Little Quee

Once there was a boy
    called Little Quee,
    who lived in a house of snow.
He had no mother or father,
    but he had a grandmother
    who looked after him.
She looked after him so well
    that Little Quee
    did not find out
    how to look after himself.

When he wanted something,
Grandmother was there
to give it to him.

When he fell over,
Grandmother was there
to help him up,
and Little Quee
did not find out
how to look after himself.

But one day
Grandmother had a bad leg,
and could not walk.

She could only
hop to the door
of the house of snow.

She could only
sit in the sun
and look at Little Quee.

So Grandmother said
  to Little Quee,
" Little Quee, you may play
  near the house of snow,
  but you must not go too near
  to the cold, green sea."

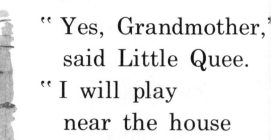

" Yes, Grandmother,"
  said Little Quee.
" I will play
  near the house
  of snow,
  and I will not
  go too near
  to the cold,
  green sea."

Little Quee played
  near the house of snow
  for a long time.
He did not go too near
  to the cold, green sea.

He made a snow baby.
He made a snow ball.
He made a snow bear.
And Grandmother looked at him
  all the time.

Soon Grandmother fell asleep.
Then Little Quee forgot
  what Grandmother had said.
And he went very near
  to the cold, green sea.

He began to play
on the ice,
very near
to the cold,
green sea.

Then there was a crack,
a crack, crack, crack,
a very big crack in the ice.

" Oh ! " cried Little Quee.
" There is a crack in the ice ! "

The bit of ice
where Little Quee was sitting
sailed away like a boat,
with Little Quee on it.

Then Little Quee was afraid.
" Grandmother !
Grandmother ! " he cried.

" I am going out to sea !
Come and help me.
Come and help me."

Then Grandmother looked up.
She saw Little Quee
  standing on the ice.

She saw the ice
  as it sailed on the sea.

" Oh, Little Quee," she cried.
" I have a bad leg.
I cannot come and help you."

Then Little Quee cried,
" Grandmother, Grandmother,
   what shall I do ? "

" Jump, Little Quee,"
   called Grandmother.
" Jump quickly, Little Quee."

So Little Quee
   jumped.

But he did not
   jump very well,
   and he fell splash
   into the cold,
   green sea.

Then Little Quee
   was afraid.
" Grandmother,
   Grandmother ! " he cried.

" I am
  in the cold,
  green sea.
Come and help me.
Come and help me."

" Oh, Little Quee,"
  cried Grandmother.
" I have a bad leg.
I cannot come and help you."

Then Little Quee was afraid.
" Grandmother, Grandmother,"
  he cried.
" What shall I do ? "

" Swim, Little Quee,"
  called Grandmother.
" Swim quickly, Little Quee."

Then Little Quee cried,
" Grandmother, Grandmother,
  how shall I swim ? "

" Pull with your arms,
  and kick with your legs,"
  called Grandmother.
" Swim, swim, Little Quee.
Swim quickly, Little Quee."

Little Quee was afraid,
  but he gave a pull
  with his arms,
  and he kicked
  with his legs,
  and he found
  that he could swim.

So he swam and swam,
and he forgot
that he was afraid.

He found
that he liked
swimming.
He liked it so much
that he did not
want to stop.

So he swam
and he swam
for fun.

But Grandmother called,
" Little Quee, Little Quee,
come out quickly
and get dry."

So Little Quee swam back
in the cold, green sea.

Then he went back
over the ice and snow.
He went back
to where Grandmother sat
at the door
of the house of snow.

" Oh, Little Quee,"
  said Grandmother.
" You went too near
  the cold, green sea.
You went much too near
  the cold, green sea.
But you are very clever
  for you can swim now."

After that
  Grandmother was afraid
  to go to sleep again.
But Little Quee
  was so tired
  that he fell asleep at once,
  lying on the snow in the sun.

Slip, the Sea Lion

Slip was a sea lion
  who was black and shining.
He lived in a pond by the sea.
The pond had a wall round it.

Every day a man came
  to give him something to eat.
Every day
  the children came to see him.

Slip was a happy sea lion,
   but sometimes he was sad
   for he did not like
   to be alone.

Sometimes he thought,
" I wish I had another sea lion
   to swim in the pond with me."

One morning
   Slip said to himself,
" I will leave the pond.
I will go out
   and look for another sea lion
   to swim in the pond
   with me."

So he swam along
   and jumped over the wall.
Splash ! He went into the sea.

Then he swam away.

He swam and he swam,
  looking for another sea lion
  to take back to the pond.

Soon the man went to the pond
  to give Slip something to eat.
But oh, Slip was not there !

Where could he be ?

Then the children
  went to the pond
  to look at Slip.
But oh, Slip
  was not there !

Where could he be ?

The man said,
" I will take
a boat.
I will go and
look for him."

So the man called
two other men,
and all three of them
went into a boat.

They sailed out to sea,
looking for Slip the sea lion,
but they could not find him.

They looked and looked
for a long time,
but still
they could not find him.

At last they saw something !
They saw a black, shining head.
They saw a sea lion
    swimming in the sea.

" Oh," said the first man.
" There is Slip the sea lion ! "

(But it was not Slip at all.
    It was another sea lion.)

The men took the boat
    nearer to the sea lion.
" Yes," said the second man.
" This sea lion
    is black and shining.
It is Slip."

(But it was not Slip at all.)

" Now," said the third man,
    " we will catch him.

We will catch Slip the sea lion."

(But it was not Slip at all.)

One man sailed the boat.
The two other men
    put their hands
    in the water
    to catch the sea lion.

" Come on, Slip," they said.

But the sea lion
    tried to swim away,
    for she was not Slip at all.

The boat went after her.
The men put their hands
  in the water again,
  and this time
  they took hold of the sea lion
  and put her in the boat.
" Now, Slip, we have got you,"
  said the three men.

(But it was not Slip at all.)

The boat sailed back
  over the sea to the pond.

The three men
  put the sea lion in the pond.
" Now Slip is home again,"
  they said.

(But it was not Slip at all.)

" Oh ! " cried the children.
" Here is Slip the sea lion.
He is back again."

(But it was not Slip at all.)

Now all this time
  Slip had been swimming
  in the sea, looking for
  a sea lion to take back
  to the pond with him.
But he could not find one.

He swam and swam,
  and he looked and looked,
  but he could not find a sea lion.

He could not find one at all.
So at last he thought,
" I cannot find a sea lion.
I will go back to my pond.
I shall have to live there
    alone after all."

So Slip the sea lion
    swam back to the pond.
He was very, very sad.

He jumped over the wall,
    and went splash into the pond.

But what did he see there ?

He saw a sea lion,
    black and shining like himself.

" Well ! " said Slip.   " How nice !
I have been looking for a sea lion
    to swim in the pond with me.
And here is one !
How very, very nice ! "

So Slip did not
    have to live
    by himself any more.
The other sea lion
    lived in the pond
    with him.
And they were
    happy ever after.

A House for Quee

" I don't want a house
     that's made of bricks.
I don't want a house
     that's made of sticks.
A house of ice
     is the house for me.
I like to be cold,"
     said little boy Quee.

The Birthday Kitten

Once there was a kitten,
   a small, white kitten.
She had no home
   and no one to look after her.

One morning in winter
   she was very cold,
   and very hungry.

" I am very cold," she thought,
   " and very hungry.
I wish I had a house to live in,
   and a nice little boy or girl
   to look after me.
I wish, I wish, I wish I did."

Then she saw
a postman,
but the postman
did not see her.

He was standing
by the door of
a house.

His bag was
on the ground
and he was going
to put some letters
in the box.

The small white kitten
    walked up to him
    and saw the bag.

" What is in here ? "
    she thought.
" I will have a look."

She peeped into the bag.

Then she walked inside it.

The postman did not see her.
He picked up the bag
    with the kitten inside it,
    and went along the road.
The kitten went bump, bump,
    bump inside the bag.

At first she was afraid,
    but after a time
    she went to sleep.

The postman walked
  down the road,
  going from house
  to house
  with letters.
The small white kitten
  was still asleep in the bag.

The postman
  went down another road,
  going from house to house
  with letters.
The small white kitten
  was still asleep in the bag.

Then the postman
   went down another road,
   and another road,
   and another road,
   going from house
   to house
   with letters.

The small white kitten
   was still asleep in the bag.

Then the postman
   came to a red house.

There were lots of letters
for the little girl
in that house.

" It looks as if
she has a birthday,"
thought the postman.

The small white kitten
was still asleep in the bag.

One of the letters was too big
to go in the box,
so the postman knocked.

The little girl and her mother
came to the door.

The small white kitten
was still asleep in the bag.

" Good morning," said the
postman.

" Good morning,"
said the mother.

" Good morning,"
said the little girl.

Then the postman said
to the little girl,
" See how many letters
I have for you today.
One, two, three, four, five, six !
There are six letters all for you.
Is it your birthday ? "

" Yes," said the little girl.
" It is my birthday.
I am six years old today."

She took the six letters
from the postman, and said,
" Thank you very much."

Then, what do you think ? —
the small white kitten
jumped out of the bag,
and into the little girl's arms !

" Oh ! " said the little girl.
" A small white kitten
   for my birthday !
That is just what I want."

Her mother laughed,
   and the postman laughed.
But the little girl
   took the kitten into the house,
   and gave her something to eat.

So the small white kitten
   was never cold
   or hungry again.

She had found
   a house
   to live in,
   and a nice
   little girl
   to look
   after her.

Dog Island

John and Peter
  went out for a walk
  with Rags, the little black dog.
They walked through the field
  and along by the river.

Rags, the little black dog,
  liked the river.
So he ran down to the edge,
  and went splash into the water.

" Bow-wow," he said.
" I am swimming."

He swam a long way.   He swam
to a small green island
in the river.

And there he played.
He ran through the grass,
and rolled on the grass.

John and Peter said,
" We will wait for him."
But Rags did not come back.

Then they called Rags, but
Rags did not come back.

He was too busy playing
on the island,
on the small green island
in the river.

John and Peter
   sat down to wait.

Then they called Rags again
   but Rags did not come back.
He was still too busy playing
   on the small green island
   in the river.

" Come," said John to Peter.
" Let us go. Rags will come
   when he is ready."

Just then it rained.
It rained and rained.

" We must run,"
said Peter.

The rain was
very heavy,
and the boys
did not want
to get wet.

So they ran home quickly.

Peter went into his house,
and John went into his house.

" Where is Rags ? "
said John's mother.

" He swam
to the small green island
in the river," said John.

" He would not come back
    when I called him."

" He will come soon," said
    Mummy.

But Rags did not come at all.

In the afternoon John said,
" Mummy, may I go
    and look for Rags ? "

" Yes, " said Mummy.

So John called for Peter,
    and they both went
    to look for Rags.

The rain was over,
    but the wind
    was blowing.
It was blowing
    and blowing.

Soon John and Peter
   came to the river.

The water was
   running fast.

It was splashing,
   splashing,
   splashing high.

The boys could see Rags.
He was sitting
   on the small green island
   in the river.
He was looking at the water,
   but he was afraid to swim.

The water was running too fast.
It was splashing,
   splashing too high.

" Rags cannot swim in this,"
   said John.

" The wind is blowing too hard,
and the water
is running too fast
and splashing too high."

" No," said Peter.

" He cannot swim in this.
Let us go to the boatman
and say,
' Please, will you take a boat
and get Rags for us '."

So they went to the boatman.

" Please," said John.   " My dog
   is on the small green island
   in the river,
   and he cannot swim back.
Please, will you take a boat
   and get him for us ? "

" No," said the boatman.
" I cannot take a boat
   out in this.
The wind is blowing hard,
   and the water
   is running too fast.
I cannot get your dog
   for you today."

" Oh," said John.   " Rags will
   have to be there all night.
He will be very hungry."

" Yes," said Peter.
" I am afraid
  he will be
  very hungry."

Then the boatman said,
" You could throw
  some bread and meat
  over to him.
It is not very far."

" So I could," said John.

He ran home quickly,
  and came back
  with some bread and meat.
Then he went to the river
  and threw a bit of bread.

He threw
    as far as he could throw.

Splash !
The bread fell in
    the water.

" I cannot throw very far,"
    he said. " You try, Peter."

So Peter tried.
He threw a bit of bread
as far as he could throw.

Splash !
The bread fell in the water.

" I cannot throw
very far,"
said Peter.
" I will try to throw
some meat."

He threw
a bit of meat
as far as he could,
but that fell
in the river too.

" Let us go to the boatman
and see if he will try."

So then the boatman
tried to throw
a bit of bread.

He threw it so far
that it fell
on the small green island
in the river.

It fell near to Rags,
the little black dog,
and Rags ate it at once.

Then the boatman threw
all the bread and all the meat
over the river to hungry Rags.

" Now he will eat
the bread and meat
and he will not be hungry,"
said the boatman.

85

" Thank you,"
said John and Peter.
" Thank you very much
for your help."

So Rags was on the island
all night,
but he was not hungry.

Next morning the wind
was not blowing so hard,
and the water
was not running so fast
or splashing so high.

Rags looked at the river,
and thought,
" Now I can swim back."
So he jumped into the river
and swam back.

Then he ran through the field
and went home.

" Here I am,"
he tried to say to John.

John was very happy
to see Rags again,
and he ran out to tell Peter
that Rags had come home.

Peter was happy too.
" Now we will call the island
' Dog Island '," he said.

So John and Peter
and all
the other children
called the island
" Dog Island "
ever after.

Things To Do
What Are They ?

We are red.
We are Sally's.
She puts us on for dancing on Saturdays.
  What are we ?

I am cold and thick.
I am on the pond.
The brave little duck made a hole in me.
  What am I ?

I have water all round me.
I am in the river.
Rags, the little black dog,
  stayed on me all night.
    What am I ?

The man threw me for the children
  to catch.
I am round and silver.
I sailed on the sea all night.
  What am I ?

The old man and woman had me.
I was left in the box on the table.
I could give them one wish.
What am I ?

I am green and cold.
Little Quee fell into me.
He liked swimming in me.
What am I ?

The postman did not see me in his bag.
I was hungry and small.
Now a little girl looks after me.
What am I ?

I am a sea lion.
I live in a pond.
I went to look for another sea lion.
What is my name ?

I swam to a small green island.
The boatman threw me some bread
and meat.
I am John's dog.
What is my name ?

Things To Draw

Draw Little Quee
  and his grandmother
  standing in the snow
  outside their house of ice.
Draw a sea lion
  swimming in the sea.
Make the sea look green and cold.

Look back at the story
  called " The Magic Ring,"
  and draw all the things
  the old man and his wife bought.
Then draw a box
  to keep the magic ring in,
  and a table to put it on.

Draw the dog called Rags,
  and draw some bread and meat
  for him to eat.
Draw the river splashing high
  and the small green island.
Draw John and Peter.
Draw the man and his boat.

Word List

This list shows all the new words (73) in Playbook 3 other than derivatives from words already known (e.g. brings, sitting). All the remaining words in the book have already occurred in Book 3 or in earlier stages of the Happy Venture reading scheme. The numbers refer to the pages on which the words first appear.

1 brave wind	25 smiled their	48 quickly splash
2 leave	26 tried	50 arms
3 grass	28 sailed boat just Peter	51 swam
4 more		53 clever tired lying
7 thicker		
8 another swimming	29 night	54 slip lion every
9 left fine	30 nearer	
	32 magic wife only	55 alone
10 shining		63 ever
11 girls	33 work hard buy	64 that's
13 gone		65 hungry
14 green trot		67 inside
	34 bought	70 knocked
15 dancing	37 cart	72 years
16 nice	40 never	74 island Rags through edge
17 back once	42 Quee lived himself	
18 picked		
22 sea	45 forgot	77 rained
23 held	46 crack afraid	78 both
24 dollar John should		82 far

OLIVER & BOYD
Tweeddale Court
14 High Street
Edinburgh EH1 1YL
(A Division of Longman Group Limited)

First Published 1954
Second Edition 1963
Revised Edition 1971
Second Impression 1972

ISBN 0 05 002386 1

Printed in Hong Kong by
Dai Nippon Printing Co. (International) Ltd.